Heart's
MIgratIon

Poems by
Linda
Rodriguez

TIA CHUCHA PRESS
LOS ANGELES

Printed in the United States of America
ISBN 978-1-882688-37-1

Book Design: Jane Brunette
Cover Art: "Heart's Migration," by José Faus

PUBLISHED BY:
Tia Chucha Press
A Project of Tia Chucha's Centro Cultural, Inc.
PO Box 328
San Fernando, CA 91341
www.tiachucha.com

DISTRIBUTED BY:
Northwestern University Press
Chicago Distribution Center
11030 South Langley Avenue
Chicago, IL 60628

Tia Chucha Press is the publishing wing of Tia Chucha's Centro Cultural, Inc., a 501 (c) 3 non-profit corporation. Tia Chucha's Centro Cultural has received funding from the National Endowment for the Arts, the California Arts Council, Los Angeles County Arts Commission, Los Angeles Department of Cultural Affairs, Los Angeles Community Redevelopment Agency, the Annenberg Foundation, Thrill Hill Foundation, the Center for Cultural Innovation, the Middleton Foundation, the Panta Rhea Foundation, the Attias Family Foundation, Not Just Us Foundation, the Liberty Hill Foundation, Youth Can Service, Toyota Sales, Solidago Foundation, and other grants as well as donations from Bruce Springsteen, John Densmore, Lou Adler, Richard Foos, Adrienne Rich, Tom Hayden, Dave Marsh, Mel Gilman, Denise Chávez and John Randall of the Border Book Festival, Luis & Trini Rodríguez, among others.

TABLE OF CONTENTS

one

four

To Ben,
who never stops
believing in me

A PHOENIX, SHE MOVES FROM LIFE TO LIFE

and leaves only the ashes of her old self
behind. She plunges into the dark
future from the glare of her funeral pyre
that brightens the sky of her past
for miles and years and leaves a legend
told to generations of children
of a vast golden one whose gleaming
body rose from the burning corpse,
blotting out the moon
with huge wings beating against
the burning air to lift the dead
ground to the living night sky
and fly through the moon
to a new place with new people
where she could be new herself—
until the destroyer strikes again.

Like a hunting eagle,
she lands, claws outstretched,
golden crest and feathers lost
in transit, her wings already disappearing.
She grows backward, smaller.
Now she can only crawl
into and out of shallow holes
in the ground of this new life.
Still, the wise avoid trampling her
for they know
she drags death behind her.

MEETING HECATE

How I fear the witch in me,
the one in touch
with power, the one who knows
without knowing
how, the secret
priestess, spirit-bearer, the ugly side
of woman, the crone—
and I remember the Cherokee
legend of Stoneskin, superhuman
cannibal, devouring whole
villages, how the People saw him coming
and set up a fortress of women
menstruating, how the sight
of each weakened Stoneskin
until he died and, dying, told them
all the secrets, ways
of power, conjure spells, ways
to do things.

The Cherokee live
off the wisdom
of a dying monster and the power
of bleeding women, and they remember
this. There is a witch somewhere
in every woman.

CALL ME PERSEPHONE.

They wrote it down all wrong
and backward, those Greeks.
We must seek the Great Mother
within. Driven underground,
She waits with snakes
circling wrists and waist,
constantly reborn and self-
nourishing. She will take me
into Her great lap and shelter me
from the weapons and machines of men.

Dreaming, I will rest and shed my skin,
become whole when I was seed
before I slept in the deep chanting
of the Mother's heart
and the song of Her blood.
When She spills me from Her,
I will take my newborn child and climb
to the surface like an underground spring,
welling up to green the parched earth
and fill the corn.

Outside once more,
I will hum my Mother's song with the bees
and dance in the moon among my herbs
and trees and long for time to return.
My child shall follow me and hide to watch,
cheek pressed against rough bark,
see me snake into the ground,
seeking once again within.

CHANGE OF GODS

We must be the only ones left.
All I have seen for days is death,
piled around the doors of buildings,
around the wrecked cars, bodies
like driftwood flung on the beach
after a storm. You are the first life
I have looked on, except in mirrors.
Must we not cling to each other
among these drifts of dead?
Add life to life in the ebb of backwaters,
the aftermath or the beginning,
a sinking backward or a becoming?

When we declared our god dead,
should we not have expected the old ones
to reclaim the world,
seeking burnt flesh on temple altars,
disguising their power to test hospitality
like Jupiter and Mercury in that town in Phrygia?
Have you, too, seen white horses
distant in the froth of waves?
Heard hooves rock the ocean
floor? The elements speak so clearly
now in the silence.
Let me draw you to the high ground.
See, the waters everywhere are rising.

FIRE IS THE OLDEST WILD THING

But watch the candles burn,
tamed and housebroken,
blossom-yellow flames shading
into autumn's orange and the open sky's
blue like festive streamers above the birthday cake.

In silence and solitude, however,
you can see that the bright flickering
colors surround and enclose a dark core
at the point of burn, igniting
the twisted wick's transformation
from fiber to fire.
At the heart of every dancing flame,
a piece of cold midnight.

Most people never see.
They pass through accepting
what flickers on the surface.
You must observe intently
to see and know
the black seed of holocaust
in each gay dance of domesticated flame.

THE AMAZON RIVER DOLPHIN

The sudden pink shape
surfacing in black-water lagoons
shocked explorers.
All dolphins share man's
thumb and fingerbones,
but these also wear his flesh.
When the river overflows
and floods the *varzea*,
these dolphins travel miles
to splash in the shallows
amongst buttress-roots of giant
rainforest trees.
The waters abate, trapping fish,
dolphins never.

A lamp burning dolphin oil
blinds. At night
the pink-flesh contours melt and blur.
The flipper extends the hidden hand
to lift its woman's torso
to the land. An Eve,
born each night from the black Amazon,
roams the dark banks for victims
to draw to the water and death.
Taboo to the Indians,
this pink daughter of the river's magic
always looks, to explorers,
like she's smiling.

WHEN SHE BLEEDS

rain falls on cracked soil
soaking the buried kernel
until its casing bursts
with roots and pallid stem
lifting the closed hands of new green
to the surface to burst into sultry air
with the force of all sun-seeking
life.

When she bleeds,
winter is banished and birds
build nests in chimneys
and morning enters on a coach
of song and sun and color
returns to the winter-sere sky
and warms the winter hearts of stones
so snakes can coil upon them to nap
in the sun.

When she bleeds, Persephone
rejoins her mother goddess
and the surface world for one brief
moment of light so dazzling
it blinds her, used to the eternal
darkness as she is now that she's married,
but she looks anyway, with tears
burning her eyes, at movement and sound
and life springing up at every drop
of her mother's blood.

WATER FROM THE MOON

[after *The Year of Living Dangerously*]

"All is clouded by desire,
as by dust a mirror,
as by smoke a fire:
a film of selfishness
shrouding the whole
of spirit-self,
blinding the soul."
So speaks Krishna
to Arjuna, god to prince,
puppets both.

In the *wi-yang*
watch the sacred shadow puppets.
They are souls
and the screen is heaven,
the puppetmaster priest,
in Java, land of the unseen
around us like a mist
ocean to swim through
to reach the West.

Hunger passes overhead
like a heavy cloud
on its way to drop monsoon torrents
on refugees and summer-suited diplomats,
a fleeting shadow
darkening this day with the threat
of what will come
to pass tomorrow.

Never watch the puppets,
only their reflected souls on the screen,
constant conflict right with left,
light and dark struggling
to an Eastern balance.
Even Arjuna, noble hero,
can be fickle,
betray his princess and his people
in a moment uncaring selfish.
We want answers in the West —
solutions.
In the *wi-yang* none
exist, no end arrives.
We seek the unobtainable,
water from the moon,
unable to understand 'never'
as answer,
mask ourselves in manufactured
certainties, feign strength and hide,
despise Oriental illusion.

Could we ever learn,
my shadow Arjuna, to open ourselves
to the need for love
around us like a watery envelope?
All my desire is useless,
used-up, futile.
Your smokescreen,
Arjuna, veils your heart
from mine, put on display for crowds
of callous foreigners.
I could be your eyes,
my unmet love, and make you see.
We could pool our light,
break through the clouds

that separate hearts
in the shadows
on this *maya*-moment's screen.

The crowds applaud, depart
for tumbling tin-roof shacks,
filled with laughter
of sweating children among the squalor.
Our purses, fatter
than any eldest daughter,
hide us from each other
as we pass in the street's steam.
The West owns the world
and I would give it away
to find the spirit-path to you,
Arjuna, and your air-conditioned heart.

Step into my love's sight,
dark prince, enfleshed
lord, lover of light.
Bring back the noonday sun,
ending fierce Indra's night *raga*,
and mix our souls,
after *maya*.

---

wi-yang: the sacred hindu puppet theater of Java (Indonesia)

maya: in Hinduism, the illusion of time and space that we consider life,
after which the individual soul is reunited with the universal soul.

raga: a sacred melody with its own ethical, emotional, temporal properties;
traditionally, a night *raga*, skillfully sung at noon, could produce darkness

LAMENT OF A FAILED ACOLYTE

Desperation can come from having nothing but God to love.
—MICHAEL HEFFERNAN

Desperation I've a long acquaintance with.
Desperation and hope
have been the twin pillars
between which I've sailed,
trying to avoid being eaten alive
or sucked in,
aiming at the narrow gate
sometimes called Jesus
who's run me aground on hope.
Unlike despair, hope's not a sin
against the Holy Spirit but only
against logic and forty years' experience
wandering in this hungry desert,
waiting for white wafers of grace
to descend and bring another presence.
If I sound mad, it's no wonder,
in this shaggy, lice-ridden skin
with blood of locusts on my tongue.
My big mistake was asking
I AM
in for company.
Avoid divine guests, I say
now, drowning in painful, terrifying love.
There's been a mix-up somewhere.
I put in a request for ecstasy,
not passion.

IN THE DARK OF THE YEAR

when driven inside, my mind
blooms and spreads like blood
staining water.
Season, weather,
health, all
at the bottom
of time's wheel, all
coalesce to force me inward.
Following invisible marks,
I set out stalking visions.

Traveling silent
through the trackless deep
within, beyond word, thought,
memory, beyond image,
to a region so dark
what moves within is perceived
only as a sense of lessening or deepening
of night, flaring across the void
or rippling out from corners.
This is always a trek
made against fear,
fear of losing my way, of being
trapped within, fear of being
pulled down into the void
by invisible hands, of not making it
back to the surface alive.

How many times I've ridden
the year's wheel to this base point,
yet I'm always stunned to find myself

on the subterranean trail
once more. You would think
I'd be prepared for it
after all these missions,
but it's the nature of the quest
that I must go empty-handed,
no preparations, no protection,
eternally snared by surprise.
I aspire to a vision
of an eagle, a bear,
nobility and strength. Instead
I bring back stinging scorpions,
ancient spiders, black as night,
once, a snakeskin, like jewels
with all the life exhausted.

I have heard the brittle cry of the phoenix.
Though it leads me
into hidden depths
at every turn,
I have not seen it,
even from the corner of my eye, a flash
of night, deeper, darker,
more dazzling than the inky center of my self.

SHE TAKES HER POWER IN HER OWN HANDS

and pours it over her body,
drenching hair and face,
standing in pools of herself,
dripping excess. She takes up her power
with strong hands and holds it close
to her breasts like an infant, warming it
with her own heat. She draws her power
around her like a hand-loomed shawl,
a cloak to keep the wind out,
pulling it tighter, tugging and patting it
smooth against the winter.
She pulls her power from branches
of dead trees where it has hung so long
neglected that it has changed from white to deep
weathered gold. She wraps her hair
in power like the light of distant stars,
gleaming through the dark emptiness
in and around everything. She lets her power down
into a dank well, down and down,
clanking against stone walls, until
she hears the splash, a little further
to submerge it completely, then draws it
hand over rubbed-raw hand, heavy enough
to make her shoulders and forearms ache
and shudder with strain, pulls it up
overflowing, her power,
and drinks in deep, desperate gulps
out of a lifetime of thirst. She weaves her power
into a web, a cloth, a shroud, and hangs it
across the night where it catches the light of stars
and refracts it into a shining glory,

brighter than the moon
and colder. She holds her power
in her hands at the top of the hill
in the top of the tree where she steps out
onto the air and her wings
of power buoy her to ride the thermals
higher and higher toward the sun,
her new friend.
When she returns,
she folds her power over and over
into a tiny, dense pellet to swallow,
feeling its mass sink to her center
and explode, spreading throughout to transform
her into something elemental,
a star,
a mountain,
a river,
a god.

THE ONLY WOMAN POET

I encountered, growing up,
was St. Emily Dickinson
the White. I hated her.
She seemed to say
if you want to write
poetry, great poetry,
you have to talk soft and sweet,
wear white, hide
in the house like a coffin,
never have a life, bind
your personality tight when young and live through
agonies of stunted bones and marrow
so you can be
carried around by male critics and poets
on a white pillow, suitably
and decoratively and appropriately
crippled.
The mandarins loved her.
I hated her.

Only when I grew
did I realize
how she had fooled
the imperial bureaucracy of literature,
little crippled white
girl on her fluffy, lace-trimmed white
pillow, lisping like a child
on meeting any of the mandarins,
lily in her hand, and pouring
great gouts of blood all over the page
when she was left alone and harmless. They thought

they'd made her safe, they thought
they'd made her tame and tidy, a little songbird
to sit on their manly fingers when called.
She was a hawk
with laser eyes,
a cruel curved beak,
wings of unimaginable strength,
and the raptor's instinct to distinguish
the small lives below
and drag the one she wants into the air,
kicking, squealing, bleeding.

For millennia, men have feared
the power of women bleeding.
They set up rituals to contain and weaken
that blood, spoke and wrote of such power
as unclean and cursed. They forced us
to inhibit it, hide it, deny it, be ashamed.
And Emily, dutiful daughter,
only safe woman poet,
spills her power all over the delicate rice paper,
hiding it like invisible red ink brushstrokes
in washes of weakness and white.

KATHERINE ANNE PORTER, IMPLACABLE

lady of the dry Texas fields,
you scrubbed off your country name
for the richer sound of Grandma's Katherine
when you scrapped your first husband
and took three more men
to various wedding beds.
(What did you scrape off with each of them?)
Was your life of love affairs and writing
a fool's voyage outward, stripping
constantly till in the end
you gleamed like those jewel-toned pebbles
in your Colorado River dreams?

They say you were a hard woman,
promiscuous, rebellious, a closet moralist.
Instead, were you Miranda,
betrayed by memory
and corrupted by this brave new world?
Flinty with the need to create, you
became the shadow of a great rock
in that tired Texas desert.
Kallie, you deserved
your grandmother's stolen name.

IT'S SNOWING IN KANSAS CITY, VIRGINIA WOOLF,

and what would you think
of my city and my snow
(for I possess both)
and my day, when some of your dreams
have come true for some women,
but far from all of them
(dreams or women).
I think you would like
our women writers, even the ones
you didn't think were very good.
You would like them for being
writers and for trying and
for their very number and variety.
And since you are dead and thus
also belong to me in a way, as I choose
to learn about your life, to know you,
I think you would like the things
I like and dislike what I dislike.
Not fair to you, perhaps,
but if you'd wanted better,
you should have stuck around.
You should have lived forever,
Virginia, or at least long enough
to see the snow fall
out of a bright, gray sky
and stick to ice-coated leaves
and branches and eaves and power lines
in Kansas City and tell me
what you think of it all.

JOANNE'S BRAIN

Joanne's hands shake now.
She forgets what she meant to say,
disconnects a caller.
Packs of white dogs menaced
the car she no longer drives.
Bumblebees the size of her fist
clamored at her window.

Epilepsy is a word
no one wants to speak.
Insurance can be denied.
Employers turn away.
Joanne insists on naming it,
explaining it to professors, friends,
family, all afraid to hear.
Dilantin keeps her seizures at bay—
most months—but they lurk
in a spot on the left side of her skull.
She's lost trust in her own brain.
One morning, a red fox
ran across the grounds
outside our office. Only Joanne
thought it hallucination.

When I was growing up,
I watched my stepfather's body
arch and bounce on the floor,
grand mal seizures, his.
Larger than my tiny mother,
I helped him up
to the couch after,

while Mom brought wet washcloth,
dry towel to clean the drool
from his decent face. His family turned away
after the first seizure when he lost college
money a semester before his degree.

I know epilepsy
through him. I leave my child with Joanne
when I go to night classes,
know the hounds
that stem from Joanne's brain
will harm no one.

DREAMING OF MY LATE MOTHER-IN-LAW'S HOUSE

Smelling the sharp incense,
cumin and jalapeños,
I cross her floors
again, gold and white shag leading
past couch-flowers.
The television, an altar, always holds
fourteen family faces,
purple candles and Our Lady
of Guadalupe.

In the dining room,
Christ, crucified,
oversees holiday feasts,
and the corner between two doorways
holds the celebrant's chair
with gilded legs. Her sight
stolen by diabetes, Jennie
swivels—never rocks—from voice to voice,
answering with a high laugh like a child's
in an empty choirloft,
offering counsel and comfort
with a flutter of dove-plump hands.

Thermostats set at eighty
make sleep slow to come
in her high beds
while dried palm fronds, blessed
on Passion Sunday,
rattle against the lintels
and hold our city souls
inviolate
in that sacramental house
sanctified by holy water and her.

MAKING ENCHILADAS

We set up an assembly line.
I heat the tortillas in *manteca*
after Crystal dips them in *chile ancho*
and drains them. Niles carries full plates
of hot tortillas to his father,
who rolls them around spoonfuls of filling.
When we've finished the hot, greasy work,
I pour the last of the sauce over neat rows
of stuffed tortillas, sprinkle them with cheese,
clean the stove and counters.
The kids help their father rinse plates and pans.
They don't know this is the last time.
The cheese melts. Crystal
dances to "No More Lonely Nights" on the radio.
Niles and his dad joke and wrestle.
After grace, we sit before steaming plates.
The kids stuff their mouths, insult each other,
and laugh. We can't avoid their eyes
forever. Their father and I stare
at each other across the table.

TELLING THE KIDS

We've put it off
as long as we can,
trying to memorize this ourselves
before we pass it on —
oral teaching, blurred boundaries
drawn in the dirt with sticks —
to the young woman who looks like me
and the boy already taller than you.
For weeks, they've sensed a changing
in the outlines of their world
and closed ears and eyes
to continue with hands clutching our clothes
as when they were toddlers,
early in the journey
when we still knew the land.

You and I have had no time
to map this unexpected territory
that stretches before us
in brand-new blackness.
We all have to find our own
path through this. They can't
just follow us anymore.
We're stumbling in opposite directions.

GLENDA'S PRESCRIPTION

"Have a cup of tea, Madame Bovary,"
she says, poking fun at Flaubert's doctor
to remind me life doesn't care
about minor tragedies, funerals of love.
Life doesn't even slow down for a look
when the big black cars lead
the procession from the chapel.
Traffic only halts long enough by law
to keep the grieving concentrated.
No consideration for stragglers
who must fight rush hour
like everyone else and hope
they make it before the last amen.
"Just make it hot and put lots of sugar in,"
she says with a practiced mourner's smile.

SELF-PORTRAIT AS ORPHEUS AND EURYDICE

Knowing his music was empty without her,
he had to dive into those dark waters
from which none returned except as flotsam,
crustacean-nibbled and bloated with the gases of decay.
How long he hesitated, songless but safe,
on the bank. She watched him decide
through the eternal minutes of her dreading
that he could decide
to abandon the notes shimmering in the air
around his head, ignore that nimbus of power
from beauty, and walk mute
through an ordinary life. She waited in fear
until he threw himself into the waves and sank
without struggle.

Almost out, he could feel her behind him
like an insistent melody pushing through his fingers
to reach the strings. He was so full of the moment,
his greatest song, bringing her back.
Such power—who knew what he could do?
He wanted to see the wonder in her eyes,
needed the perfect last note,
pure and silvery and light as bone,
the end of sound.

SELF-PORTRAIT AS ADAM

She has always been there, mother
of the world, saying stop and be conscious
of your net of relation with the earth and others
and her, always tying me down,
holding me back, heavy
and aware and of the very dirt
I shake from my sandals and shoes
and build and amass and use
and destroy and waste and kill
and do, always do, drugged by action.
Don't ask me to be
anything. I am what I do; I am
because I do. I force change
on everything. I cannot, will not
change myself. She must understand.
I am what I am.
Where have I heard that before?

SELF-PORTRAIT AS EVE

I am the first awake, a clod
of dirt held together with divine spit,
alone in consciousness. When you wake beside me,
I am so grateful for the company
that I will spend life after life,
dreaming of that shared moment,
waiting for you to join me in awareness.
You will decide I was too needy
and must be an inferior part of yourself,
for you have never spent that eternity alone and aware
without me, don't understand
the welcome you received
as if a god. You will demand
worship and sacrifice and hold me
responsible for our expulsion
from the mindless garden of the beasts.
I see myself as earth; you see yourself as god-like.
I go along for centuries until I begin
again to long for that moment alone
among sleeping animals.

SELF-PORTRAIT AS ISIS

I found a thigh last night.
That makes a pair. All I need
for the lower half, now, is one foot,
the left, I believe —
it's hard to remember
after all these years.
When I have that,
plus the groin,
I'll have it all.
(I carry the head with me in a bag
hung from my belt.
I've had to find it twice, so
I'm taking no chances.)
There's something I must do
with all these parts.
They add up somehow
to something more, a whole,
a self of some kind. I can't recall
if it's mine or someone else's.
I'm working to complete a person —
I don't know who any longer.
Never mind.
When I have it all,
I'll remember.

WISDOM IS THE FEMININE FACE OF GOD,

like snow. Her white robe surprises us
with its soft, cold fabric
outlining every tree
and fence in harsh silhouette.
Wisdom falls softly and
steadily when conditions are ripe
and accumulates in silence, transforming
iron-barred, graffiti-marred neighborhoods
into landscapes fit for the best suburban walls.
Wisdom never worries about respectability,
cares nothing for the worth
of what lies beneath her skirts.
Wisdom loves radiance and brings it
out in the most startling spots. Wisdom turns
making-do into unmarred beauty
that was always there
behind the everyday — God the housewife.

CONSIDERING OCEANS

I

Inside the museum this sultry afternoon,
the air-conditioned hum offers an imitation
peace like that of libraries and empty churches.
I wait for you, as I have promised,
promising myself this afternoon will do no damage
to an earlier oath, watching out the window
where the sun shatters
against the fountain's water and water
transmutes to something other than air or water.
Though I sit at the point of betrayal,
my face feels smooth and unyielding
as the face of Saint Teresa
gilded on peeling wood or the sea
on the wall before me, becalmed yet broken
by the ship's hull and dorsal fins.
The ocean next to that one is all drowning
storm and cloud, as if the two paintings were
before and after, the seeds of one
hidden in the other.

II

Must it always be one or the other?
My husband's love laps at my closed shore,
then slides back into turquoise depths, a lake
his love, no sea like yours,
gray ocean breakers rolling over
galleons and frigates and the backs of whales
and sharks and squid and dolphins who
leap and squeal as they follow the sails

of men (and now their motors), catching rides
on the wakes of ships. He has no dolphins
in him, only freshwater fish, frogs and trees
under the water, a sunken forest
drowned with its squirrels, snakes, ants and bees
that once made a world, reduced
to a floating green crest.

III

We whisper in deep-carved shadows
of the recreated medieval chapel.
They built to keep the heat and sun out.
The dark ages knew
summer draws insanity and sin,
a poultice pulling infection from the soul
to burst in the sun.
It was always summer in Eden.

IV

Mother of Perpetual Help,
with your slanted eyes hurt
by visions of your later Son
who sits now, infant, in your hand, a perfect
fit, and takes your thumb
between his palms, as if to suck,
pray for us.

Mother of the Word Incarnate,
though attended by angels
floating near your narrow ears,
though surrounded by hieroglyphics
and striped everywhere,

your Son as well, with gold,
though you wear a halo crown,
despise not our petitions.

Virgin of Virgins,
in paint, wood, song, stone, clay,
I stand before this incarnation
with its blue porcelain necklace
and long hands that cup your Infant
as if you would never let go.
Help us, we pray.

V
We enter the twentieth century
on the floor above. Neon tubes,
gears and ratchets, kinetic
sculptures flashing dissonance,
disjointed collage, counterfeit
museum guard so real
you ask for directions to the men's room,
have to get them from the small black
woman in uniform in the corner.
I turn back,
down the marble stairs,
run through the Egyptians
all the way to the Coptics, hide
among flat-faced icons, holding my breath
from fear of your finding me,
of what I will want to do
if you do. I watch you pass the massive stone
lion-casket on your way out.
I breathe again
in pain.

VI

In these halls of art, Mother,
I call on you with your human face
and divine Lover who came
only once, leaving you to someone else's
kindness. I can see how hard
your life must have been with him
always forgiving.
Yet he loved the boy.
Of course, you were innocent,
they say, and angels smoothed
your way with Joseph afterward. None of them
will come to my husband, asleep,
to tell him I've escaped burning
but not the ocean.

VII

Am I any less lost in the storm
because it has a frame?
The Englishman who laid down
the paint so long ago felt
the lash of rain, shivered to thunder's
blast, saw lightning burn
its way across the clouds to the sea,
even if he stood before a tea table
on floral carpet as he splashed ocean
across canvas. His tempest rages before me
six generations later. Drenched,
I wander home.

BLAME IT ON SUMMER

that I smile too widely,
grinning really, and laugh
too loud and often; that I walk
with spring and sensual sway;
that I stretch myself and twist
like a cat
baking in the backyard
brightness; that my brain is sun-bleached,
all rule and thought boiled away, leaving
only sensory steam;
that my feverish eyes see strange dancing
flames in afternoon shadows
along the sides of streets and Bedouin oases, fragrant
with dates and goats and acrid desert waters,
in every suburban garden we pass
while you argue and drive
and I stare, heavy-brained with heat
and too aware of my own body
and every other;
that I take a lover,
brazenly, crazily,
too sun-stupid to be careful,
in my dreams.

STEELING MYSELF

Afterward,
I sit up in bed, shaking.
This was my last try.
He doesn't know,
wants to go on
pretending I sleep.
The tears in his voice will try to soften
my back, but I've learned
the way those tears vanish
into his hip pocket
once I bend.
Staring ahead into the dark,
I shiver and start
to say everything
I'd decided not to say.

AFTER DINNER UNDER VAN GOGH'S "STARRY NIGHT"

This night is something new,
a sudden gift—your skin
soft against my face,
taking me by surprise.
Around all this burning, the sky
swirls in bursts of distant light.
The ricocheting, somersaulting stars
watch me shake and whisper words
I can't remember
once they've passed my lips.
I pull back my face and see
the night as Vincent saw it,
a blinding tarantella.

Your hands arc and spiral
across my back, burning
through skin and muscle to the spine.
I trace your features
like a blind woman trying to see
this stranger behind the face
I know. Vincent knew this night
where we touch as lovers
before we say our last good-bye
as friends.

CAVEAT EMPTOR

This is serious business.
I can't pretend to you.
I discard window dressing,
displaying all of me before you.
Not trying to hide
or fix up flaws, from stretch marks to scars
of old loves.
Everything inside me—
from bones to dreams—
has been cracked and mended.
I'm an honest woman,
want no cheating.
Take a good long look.
We can't have any dissembling,
no pride or shame between us, love.
This is for real.

IN THE BEGINNING

we spiral off
star, moon and wintry sun
from our conjunction,
lighting an empty globe,
that collision of traveling bodies, their heat
drawing forth
from chaos fish, birds, beasts that crawl,
from the still, breathless point.

Together in the cooling afterworld,
we swallow fruits, tubers, grubs, in vain
attempts to stay warm
in separate skins, seeking
the shelter of caves.

SKIN HUNGER

forgive me for touching so much
my hand
cupping your ear
stroking the planes of your jaw
caressing your hair
warming the nape of your neck
sliding down your arm from the shoulder
while we talk
I can't help myself
you are a warm room with fireplace
table laid for supper
couch and soft coverlets
I have been sleeping so long
a bag-lady
on cold bare floors
stealing what food I can
from garbage cans and purses
or whatever gets dropped or thrown away
in front of me
psychologists have a name
for this need
those modern Adams
making real our fears and fantasies
by the ancient magic
of naming
skin hunger
they call it

what a true naming
my skin starved for yours
hungering and thirsting

for you to slide
silky down my throat
fill my emptinesses
warm my insides
stick to my ribs
preserve me from starvation gnawing
muscle   and bone
take me home
bathe me in your touch
swaddle me with your flesh

the skin is an organ
breathing for the body
warming and cooling it
thousands of nerve endings
sensory receptors
antennae stretched and rolled
thin and flexible to cover us
every trace of your fingertips
down my spine
around my shoulderblades
every caress of belly
buttock thigh ankle
sets off minute electrical charges
in the muscles
my own internal fireworks
feed my skin with your own
love
nourish me with your legs
and arms wrapped around me
find some way for us to devour
each other merging
if only for an explosive instant
into some new full creature

TO A LONE DOLPHIN

Pierce the sea's surface.
Arch your body, one long muscle,
expanding and contracting
with the changing pressure
of a liquid world.
Ride out the tempests
within, gentle
master of breaker and swell.
Fill these waters
with echoes
of your presence.
Sing songs in your strange tongue,
safe within the sea's embrace.
Dolphin, this ocean loves you.

BORN AGAIN

This has been going on for an eternity
that neither wants to end and neither thinks could last
a second longer.

She was opening and spreading through the palpable
air, out the window above the shared driveway, startling
the neighbors at their backyard grill, over the trees
covering their topmost leaves with the sparkling sweat
she left in a cloud behind her, hanging in the air
like some diaphanous dress seductively discarded.

The birds would fly in formation beside her
and answer her screaming with their own.

But he wanted to keep her as much as he wanted to
send her so high and away that she could never
again send a shudder down his back, never
make him shake from some inner
chill in the afternoon heat,
wanted to pin her down to the pillow, to the sheet,
to the mattress, to the spring, to the summer that was
this moment, needed to pin her down to him,
coalesce her dissipating particles into
matter to fill his palms, mouth, arms.

And she was afraid
of dissolving into vapor in the humid air,
searching for enough mass to form cloud,
to bring the forked
lightning to pierce her vagueness
and clap of thunder

to wake her,
calling out and crying out and speaking
in tongues, coming back from so far and long,

breathing again, pinned to the sticky sheets,
newborn,
saved,

and they lie in each other's shadows in the afternoon
sun while the neighbors glance at the sky uneasily
and cluck their tongues.

WINNING THE BATTLE

you love to make me beg
shaking with need
until finally I understand
push your hands away
and pull you onto me
surrender
like a defeated city
conquered and looted
survivors abandoning
the fighting in the streets struggling
to hide from the flames
while their homes are invaded
plundered destroyed
a ruined fortress
gates torn asunder
walls cracked open
like an overripe seed
burning in the night
ringing
with the sounds of boot
and spur the jangle
of armor and sword
jostling crowds of swaggering
conquerors marching in
pouring through forced openings
pressing forward penetrating
each dark alley hidden
storeroom filling
empty chairs and cups
splashing wine laughing
singing feasting amid ashes

taking possession
of what once resisted so fiercely
and now lies wide open

AFTER THE FINAL SCENE

In early days,
you said you liked to see
yourself as Shane forever
riding away
alone. I forced a laugh,
said I would be
the towhead child running behind
the pale horse, crying,
"Shane, come back.
Come back, Shane."
You nodded and grinned.

We are still together,
against the odds
against us. In time
we change,
push and pull,
demand and plead,
come together,
then fall
apart, only to come
to ourselves again.

We make strange sense,
you, mounted and dangerous,
me, homesteader's child
with tired legs, stubborn
voice. Sometimes
you look back, nod and grin.
Are you slowing down
or am I
growing up?

CHRISTMAS EVE MEDITATION WHILE WAITING TO PAY

Standing in shopping-center lines,
I remember last Christmas in your arms.
I dream your voice on the phone at midnight,
asking to come home,
how I will unlock the door
to admit you from the black cold
and hold you,
chilled and shaking from something
deeper than cold.
I dream you
on your knees, how I will
drop to my own and join you.

A tightmouthed woman behind me
jabs my back with a box corner,
and I step forward,
one person closer
to paying for what I want to give.

TEXT

The gesture between them
told the story—desire
and renunciation
in one unbroken move,
love as a kind of power
to be resisted. The more she opened
to him like petals unfurling,
the closer she came
to the blown bloom,
the stronger his need
to pluck and own
in order to discard
as dying. His hand pulling
her body to his and forcing
her away again without a halt
in the motion, as if one direction
inevitably
caused the other, like inhaling
causes exhaling, systole diastole,
that close and natural. That gesture
told their history and future.

ABISHAG

I want you so much
that you could close your eyes
and pretend I was whoever
you could want
while I traveled the length of you.
I would do it to hear you moan,
even knowing the sound
was for someone else.
And when you turned your back to me
to sleep, emptied,
I would hold you,
warm your always-cold frame
with my overheated skin.
Each of us would be careful
not to let the other see
or hear tears in the night.
This, in its way, is also love.

READING AT NIGHT

In the dead night's silence
the cards whisper
in my hands,
sliding against and between
each other, rip and riffle,
keeping me company.
I spread them on my bed,
making a pattern
old as Morgan and Merlin.
The Lovers crossed
by the Tower, choose
and walls come tumbling
across my tufted quilt,
the final outcome
the Hanged Man.
I sit with my back to the dark,
seeking some portent,
any sign of you,
shuffling the future
in my hands.

APACHE DANCE IN LOOSE PARK

The man and woman in the frozen park
at midnight are crazy. See
them dance—come together,
her eyes spitting, his aware of his sin.
Watch her rigid stance
melt and his slouch turn fierce.
With choreographed impulse, her hand extends
to touch his cheek. He jerks away
in pain or something rougher.
Her shoulders sag, then square
themselves and shrug. She pivots,
ready to leave. Now he reaches out,
spins her around, draws her
close. She struggles
against his arms and chest, hands fluttering, while
he drags her off the spotlit sidewalk.
Watch her glance at the dark bushes, then
at the strange hate
in his face. See how grim
her own grows, how
she tosses her head toward the night,
as if to say, "Go ahead.
Get it over with. Rape me, kill me,
end it somehow. You can't want that
any more than I do."
Now his face softens.
Once more she tries to touch.
He sways away from her outstretched fingertips.

They're crazy. Listen
to her laugh, twisting loose

and whirling away from her opponent
in the dance or war
they've staged here
where all breath is visible
under the streetlamps. How fast
she runs to her car and leaves.
How unprepared for this step he is.
He can't reach out
to stop her until her car is rolling
down the drive. In the rearview mirror,
she will see his hand lift,
his mouth open, his face twist,
and she will notice
what a stranger he is, older
and fatter and sadder
than she realized.
She will stop for coffee and doughnuts
and warmth, sit coughing and shivering
alone and hate every man
who eyes her.
He will clutch his chest
alone under the streetlamp,
bowing to the audience of tree and frost,
then stumble, suddenly blind,
to his car and drink
himself to bed, only to dream
of shrubs hiding blood and bruised flesh
on the frozen ground, of how
a man can come so close to killing
what he loves.

COYOTE, BATHED IN LIGHT

Years,
shuffling
along in black and white,
always dusk,
gritty and hopeless,
eyes to the ground,
the same round day
after day. Dust and dark
and not even despair,
just defeat.

One night, like all the others,
she walks in,
carrying the sun
inside and shining.
He has to close his eyes
against that fierce light,
and when he opens them
again, the world
around him breathes color
and life and hope,
rowan trees filled with berries
for the robins and mourning
doves and mockingbirds
filling the air
with their songs,
meadows of wildflowers —
irises, gayfeather,
sage, wild roses —
fragrances
around him like

charms in the air,
and he's standing
in a deep pool
of dawn, growing
brighter each moment
she's in his world.

COYOTE IN BLACK LEATHER

Coyote slides on black leather
over the T-shirt
that reins in biceps, shoulders, chest.
Dark jeans and biker boots cover the rest
of his long, lithe body as he invades
your everyday, suburban life
like a growl.
You avert your eyes, pretend
you don't watch
his tight, hard body, his mocking face.
You know he's bad, doesn't belong.
Besides, seeing him makes your face too
red, your breath too
short, your bones too
soft, your clothes too
tight. You pretend
not to peek, don't want him to catch you looking
at the hungry way he stares at you.
Coyote has no class.

Coyote is your secret.
You tell him it's more exciting that way.
He lifts the eyebrow bisected by a scar and stares
you into silence. He knows
you're ashamed. He thinks
you're ashamed of him.
Coyote takes you
to dangerous places.
In dark, dirty bars, he threatens drunks
and fights to protect you.
Coyote takes you

where no one else can.
Coyote takes you
where you can't admit you want to go.

OUTSIDE YOUR HOUSE AT MIDNIGHT, COYOTE

stands in shadows, only the red eye
of his cigarette showing his presence.
He watches lights in windows
downstairs and your silhouette
against curtains as you move
from room to room, readying for bed.
He grinds cigarette into the ground
with his boot, to join the others
littering the spot where he lurks,
across the street, vacant lot,
under trees along the fence line.

As you switch off lights,
room by room, and climb stairs
to your bed, Coyote moves out
of the shadows, closer to you
by a few feet more. The outer rays
of the light on the corner
catch his sharp features, golden hair,
the hunger on his face.

He watches your light click on upstairs.
Closing his eyes, Coyote can see within
your walls as you undress and slide under
covers. Tendons in his neck stand out,
rigid with tension, and he swallows his own
wanting with pain. He opens his eyes
to the dark again, watches your last light
wink out, whispers something so soft
even he won't hear, stays to witness
the vulnerability of your restless body.

Sleep. Coyote's standing watch.

THREE O'CLOCK IN THE MORNING, ALONE

Coyote wails in the far field
beside his woods.
He runs yelping,
baying among the trees,
hot on your trail
across farms and highways,
down city streets to prowl
outside your triple-locked doors.

Coyote could splinter
that wood, shatter
your windows, plunge
into your life, drag you
to his den.
He will be civilized instead,
phone you in the morning, pretend
he has left a book behind.

Coyote moves back
into his woods, voice
fading.
He dials your number
now, growls into your sleepy ear.

COYOTE AT THE POETRY READING

He walks in late,
of course,
and sits in the back row
even though he's on the program.
Coyote wraps a storm
around him like a protective shield,
wears his leather like armor,
stares the woman in business suit
and her partner in high-style casual
into dropping their eyes. Coyote
makes everyone nervous.

Whispers circle the room.
Who asked him to read?
"Must have been some woman,"
one bearded man says, with a sniff.
"A guy would have known better."
"Probably thinks it's some kind of slam,"
one professor tells another.

When they call his name,
Coyote stalks to the podium
and growls into the microphone,
while, around the room, the air
burns with after-lightning
ozone and smells of blood
and splintered bones.

AFTER DROWNING IN COYOTE'S EYES

It was so unexpected,
that hot rush
of blood and joy
filling head and chest,
a force that threatened
sanity and sight
for one brief second. His eyes
locked on yours and pulled you
into their depths, drowning
the room around you and everyone
in it. Holding your breath
without intention, you sank
to the bottom of that gaze
without preparation or classes
or equipment, losing
all sense of up or down
or how to get out alive
in this strangely glowing
new world beneath the surface
of reality, no tank or snorkel
to keep life pumping
through your heart, which sped
in panic, then slowed
until it seemed you would pass out
from anoxia or something more deadly.
It was the strength of his hands
holding yours that pulled you out,
gasping and wheezing,
into the everyday
air and sight and sound
of dishes and voices all around.

He walked you out, and your unsteady feet
rolled slightly with the deep
surging flood hidden
under the surface.

COYOTE IN HIGH SCHOOL

What is it about the bad boy,
the one in black leather
on too loud, too fast wheels,
the one we were warned against in high school?
Behind the scenes of proms and sock hops
and classes sanitized so we wouldn't catch
the germs of thought,
all the girls had dreams about that bad boy
that we couldn't even admit to ourselves
while our dates were safe white bread.

When we walked down the halls to lunch,
we knew the bad boys,
leaning against the walls
in cocky poses of insolence and threat,
were using their X-ray vision to see us
naked or—worse—in our schoolgirl underwear.
Some of us hunched over our books
and scuttled past that leering line.
Some of us stretched erect and strutted slightly
on our way beyond their limited prospects.

A classic teacher's pet,
I snuck out twice with dangerous boys,
sideswiped by the kind of temporary insanity
that catches your heart in your throat,
roller-coaster, sky-diving, over-the-falls-in-a-barrel
fear and excitement blended into one shiver.

The first, in senior year, was careful with me,
insistent on leaving the good-girl scholar a virgin.
He didn't want to hurt me, he said,
didn't want to be bad news. I didn't tell him
my father had taken care of that years earlier.
I didn't answer his phone calls after that, either.
A couple of years later, the second one took me to his room
on the back of his Harley and made love to me
all night, telling me he knew he wasn't good enough
for a girl like me, but he'd make me happy anyway.
He did that, and I avoided him thereafter.

I went with each only once,
though they were more gentle than the general run
of jocks and frat boys my friends dated.
After all, the insanity had been only temporary.
I had friends who'd stepped over the line too often
or too long and paid and paid —
as did some of us who mated with business or psych majors,
just in different ways.

Looking back, I wonder
if anyone ever warns the hard-shelled boys in leather
against the honor roll girls?

COYOTE INVADES YOUR DREAMS

You're staying clear
of him. Just because
you noticed him once
or twice doesn't mean you want
anything to do with him.
He's beneath you—
and above you and inside you
in your dreams. His mouth
drinks you deep, and you come
up empty and gasping
for air and for him. That traitor,
your body, clings to him like a life
raft in this hurricane
you're dreaming. His face
above yours loses its knowing
smile as he takes you. Again,
this night, you drown
in your own desire. Coyote
marks you as his.
You wake to the memory
of a growl.

COYOTE WINTER

The wind wolf swoops down
on this city again tonight,
and if the snow it throws
across lit streets
and whipping trees outside
my second-story window
doesn't make a blizzard in full cry,
it won't be for want
of howling.

One lone shadow man
struggles up the steep street
toward the bus stop.
Why is he out in this
alone?
Where are you?

COYOTE ON THE TELEPHONE

Coyote calls you on the phone,
asks, "Where have you been all my life?"
in a voice that climbs inside your head
and crawls down your backbone
to your hips. He asks, "When
can I see you again?" Your brain
says never, but his voice stops it
and with some other part
of your body, you reply, "Whenever
you want." Coyote laughs, low and sultry,
and you shiver, knowing
how much trouble you're in.

You call Coyote. You've sworn
you won't, not again, but your fingers
press the numbers
on their own without the brain's
supervision. Your brain's not
doing too well when Coyote
is near—or even the thought
of him. When you say, "I shouldn't
have called; I swore I wouldn't,"
he laughs that way he has
that sends your synapses flying
and your skin growing too hot
and tight for your bones
that are melting as he growls.
You know you ought to hang up
and your finger sits above
the TALK button throughout

the conversation but only pushes
it after the dial tone kicks in.

You never thought you were weak
before. Coyote's taught you
what you never wanted to learn.

COYOTE AT THE PARK

Coyote sits and waits.
He's asked you to meet him
here where you'll feel safe,
as if
anywhere were safe
with Coyote.
You spot him
as soon as you enter
through the stone arches,
all that dark shining
in the sunlight.
Teenaged girls in tight pastels
giggle and flirt
with more trouble
than they could ever handle,
and Coyote sends them
off with a wink.
He's in a good mood,
waiting for you to come
as you promised,
benevolent predator
refusing the prey
on a whim or the hope
of something better.

From behind the stone,
you watch his long lithe body
stretched on the wooden bench
as if to soak up the heat
stored in its slats,
grace unconscious

of your secret admiration.
Coyote is a contented man
today when you are expected
any moment
before he realizes
you're gone.

COYOTE AT YOUR WEDDING

He left his shotgun in the car,
though he longed to storm
through the doors and aim
a blast at the groom's head.
He has no invitation,
of course,
and hopes some fool
tries to make him leave.
He's a black-leather thunderhead
among the white flowers.
He wants to make a scene,
commit a crime, scandalize
the guests, bloody
the groom's nose, carry off
the bride kicking and screaming.

As he walks through the crowd,
the invited ones move
to give him space
as they would any predator
stalking through the church.
Trouble swirls around him,
creating a wake
of racing hearts
and choked-back squeals.
He wants
to smash the flowers,
throw food at the walls,
rip the bridesmaid's
dresses, curse the minister.

He's looking but can't find you
because you're waiting
off scene for your musical cue
to enter in procession.
Coyote drops hard
into an aisle seat
in the back row
where he can grab you
and take off when you come in reach.
He props one boot
on the back of the seat in front
to block anyone else's access
to his row. He doesn't know
he's sitting on the groom's side.

P.O.W.

I

Before I fall into the past,
I drive to the library,
thumb open a book
about the death of a child
in Greenwich Village and
plunge
back
in
time
to trash-filled rooms smelling
of milk, urine, beer and blood,
doors locked and curtains drawn
against the world,
dirty baby brother caged in a playpen,
mother nursing broken nose,
split lip, overflowing ashtray,
and father filling the room to the ceiling,
shouting drunken songs and threats
before whom I tremble and dance,
wobbly diversion, to keep away
the sound of fist against face,
bone against wall.

The book never shows
the other little brothers and sister hiding
around corners and under covers,
but I know they are there
and dance faster,
sing the songs that give him pleasure,
pay the price for their sleep

later, his hand pinching flat nipples,
thrusting between schoolgirl thighs,
as dangerous to please as to anger
the giant who holds the keys
to our family prison. Mother
has no way to keep him from me,
but I can do it for her and them.

Locked by these pages
behind enemy lines again
where I plan futile sabotage
and murder every night,
nine-year-old underground,
I read the end.
Suddenly defiant, attacked,
slammed into a wall,
sliding into coma, death
after the allies arrive,
too late, in clean uniforms so like his own
to shake their heads at the smell and mess—
the end I almost believe,
the end that chance kept at bay
long enough for me to grow and flee,
my nightmare alive on the page.

Freed too late,
I close the book,
two hours vanished,
stand and try to walk
to the front door on uncertain legs
as if nothing were wrong.
No one must know.
I look at those around me
without seeming to,
an old skill,

making sure no one can tell.
Panic pushes me to the car
where the back window reflects
a woman, the unbruised kind.

In the space of three quick breaths
I recognize myself,
slam back into adult body and life,
drive home repeating a mantra,
"Ben will never hurt me —
All men are not violent,"
reminding myself to believe the first,
to hope for the last.

II

Years later, my little sister will sleep,
pregnant, knife under her pillow,
two stepdaughters huddled
at the foot of her bed,
in case her husband
breaks through the door
again. Finally,
she escapes
with just the baby.

My daughter calls collect
from a pay phone on a New Hampshire street.
She'll stay in a shelter for battered women,
be thrown against the wall
returning to pack
for the trip back to Missouri,
a week before her second anniversary.
With her father and brother,

the trip home will take three days,
and she will call for me again.

Ana and Kay, who sat in my classes,
Vicky, who exchanged toddlers with me once a week,
Pat and Karen, who shared my work,
and two Nancys I have known,
among others,
hide marks on their bodies and memories,
while at the campus women's center
where I plan programs for women students
on professional advancement
and how to have it all,
the phone rings every week with calls we forward
to safe houses and shelters.

In my adult life, I've suffered no man
to touch me in anger,
but I sleep light.

OKLAHOMA POEM

[for Jim Barnes]

In his first words, I can hear Oklahoma,
the hill country way back behind his talk
about teaching French literature in translation,
as if I have gone home, drifted back
through all the years to that childhood place I fled.

I have described it to others
as the armpit of the nation,
when I was young and not long free
of its windy roads and redbud trees and overgrown
hills, still hurt and bitter
about things Oklahoma had little to do with,
beyond being the last place to stand
for a people and the place where one of them
was born and the place where he left
his wife and kids. The last two events were
what ate at me, and they could have
happened anywhere.

Only the first was unique
to Oklahoma, the old Indian territory
where my ancestors limped off the Trail of Tears
to join other tribes forced from their homes
by other ancestors of mine,
founded the Cherokee Female Seminary
at Tahlequah and a newspaper
all over again,
were finally forced to give up their lands
so rich ranchers could take the best parts

of the reservation and leave the hilly, scrub lands
to my great-grandparents, great-aunts, grand-uncles,
and Grandma.

What does any of this have to do with me now
all these years and miles away?
Me, with the broad squaw face,
as my father, from whom it came, called it?
When I hear Jim say about Oklahoma
(as one refugee to another), "We both got out,
but it's still inside—it settles in you,"
I know he's right, Oklahoma in more than his voice,
in the way he makes light of misfortune,
in his penchant for poking fun
at pretensions, his own and others'.
Oklahoma's settled in us both.
And through the echoes in his voice of its turtledoves
and winds and sky that could pull you off your feet
into infinity if you didn't have troubles to weigh you down
to the earth, I make my peace with it
and come home.

CONVERSATION WITH MY MOTHER'S PICTURE

You and Dad were entirely happy here —
you in purple miniskirt, white vest and tights
(you always wore what was already too young
for me), Dad in purple striped pants,
a Kansas State newsboy's cap
made for a bigger man's head.
You both held Wildcat flags and megaphones
to cheer the football team who,
like the rest of the college, despised you
middle-aged townies, arranging for their penicillin
and pregnancy tests and selling them
cameras and stereos at deep discount.
But you were happy
in this picture, before they found
oat-cells in your lungs.

After the verdict, he took you to Disneyland,
this man who married you and your five children
when I was fifteen. He took you cross-country
to visit your family, unseen
since your messy divorce.
He took you to St. Louis
and Six Flags Over Texas and to Topeka
for radiation treatments.
I don't think he ever believed
you could die. Now he's going
the same way. And none of us
live in that Wildcat town with the man
who earned his "Dad" the hard way
from suspicious kids and nursed
your last days. For me, this new dying
brings back yours, leaving me only this image
of you both cheering for lucky winners.

SAFE AT LAST

I can't cry any more,
eyes swollen, lashes stuck together,
so come then, elusive sleep,
wipe the screen behind closed lids
of today's grief. Show films
scrambled in the projector,
ends and beginnings framed
by the middle, split once
and then again, past still coming,
future remembered, present
dreamed but never known.
Mix the stilted eulogy and the trip to Disneyland.
Let him coach the scrubby little-league team
as we stand on glowing green plastic
artificial grass carpet
under the cobalt blue vinyl canopy,
listening to echoes
of his voice calling to my brother,
"Slide home. Go for it. Home."

KNITTING IN TIME OF CRISIS

Since we invaded Afghanistan and Iraq,
I've been knitting
a lot, some might say compulsively
if they were unkind.
I prefer to avoid the unkind. They are
so often aggressive, and after all,
I'm just knitting.

Simple garter-stitch scarves
of loopy, fluffy novelty yarns, long enough
to wind again and again around the neck
or tie behind the back.
Sweaters with intricate Fair Isle
patterns in parliaments of colors.
Heavy afghans of hand-spun wool
with cables twisting and winding into paths
across a snowy map.

The last time I was so knitting-obsessed,
I was trying to quit
a dangerous habit, needed
to keep my hands occupied. Now I knit
socks on tiny wooden spears, soft armor
to keep the feet of sons and nephews dry and warm.

In my sleep, I pull one loop through another
to the soft click of long bamboo sticks,
creating a whole fabric
from one long, tangled thread.

INSTINCTS

A mother possum crawled down the chimney
the spring Donny came to us
because both sets of his parents had kicked him out,
the same April after your dad and I divorced
when you kicked a hole in the dining room wall.
The possum was swollen with young
she would later carry, half-grown, on her back
or hanging from her thick, hairless tail.
"An oversized rat with maternal instincts,"
your dad once said.

Instead of one angry son, I now had two —
fifteen and seventeen —
two forged signatures on absence excuses,
two discipline committee meetings,
two conferences with the principal.
While I worked,
you shared contraband beer,
as well as the basement bedroom
with its fieldstone fireplace
in which you found the possum one cool evening.

Laughing and cheering, you teamed up
to cage her with a trash can,
carry her to the alley out back and dump her.
The possum squeezed back
down the chimney twice more. The third time
you threw her out on Troost Avenue, screaming
for a car to smash her beneath its tires.
She must have been near her time,
desperate for a nest,
to crawl back down after that.

The noise woke me after midnight.
Donny had clubbed her with his nunchuks.
You both kicked and stomped
her head as she lurched, stumbled
between your feet.
Halfway down
the basement steps I stopped,
seeing your faces. The possum fell
limp. I backed slowly up the stairs.

In the morning, you couldn't meet my eyes.
I just made you clean up the mess.

STORM SON

I almost died giving him life,
bled on the table for an hour after
his head forced its way out between my legs
while they wheeled me to the delivery room.
In fifth grade, he played football, youngest
on the field, punched holes
in the line of defense
till they tackled him and kicked in his ribs.
At sixteen, two men mugged him
on payday. He slugged the one
who took his cash. The other
slashed his arm open
before they fled. Dripping blood,
he woke me to take him for stitches.

He joined the Reserves, like most of the others
on the Fast Track in his AIT,
for college money, poor man's financial aid.
Before he joined, we talked
about war. Once an activist, I warned him
they'd call and he'd have to go.
He wasn't gung-ho, just willing to pay
the price to go to school.

When he entered college last semester,
I watched him discover
learning's delights. He planned to apply
for scholarships, decided he wanted to teach
physics, just starting
to do what I always
knew he could. Nineteen,

he looks twenty-five
to strangers who think he's my brother.
To me, he still
looks too damn young
to kill or die in the desert.

MY DAUGHTER'S NIGHTMARES

bring me nightmares. She's barely slept
for a week. I listen for tell-tale signs
behind her voice. I'm afraid
of the delicate balancing we do.
Is this the drop
too far, too hard? Should I
bring her home, cripple her further
with my caring?
Or leave her to hobble
unsupported, slowly
strengthening to just a limp—
if she doesn't fall and break
her angry neck first?

I counsel bubble bath
and bland novels. I'm wrinkled
as a prune, she replies. We both know
she needs lithium,
not lavender bath oil. She says she's
under stress. I tell her
it's the cycle,
bottoming out. She says
it's the relationship, bottoming out.
With the betraying boyfriend
or the deliberately distanced mother,
I wonder, but have no guts to ask.
You need to see someone, I say,
in despair at the depression and panic
in her voice on the pay phone.
I wait for the familiar excuses.
Silence. Yes,

she says, but how?
My breath unclenches. This
I can help with, this
I can give, a name, a phone number,
the promise of a ride.

I cannot think of her
between calls and visits, for fear
that each will be the last,
that she is too soft to survive,
that I am too hard not to.

I COULD LIVE IN THE LIBRARY,

make my bed on the floor
behind the stacks in Business & Technical,
wash in the women's restrooms,
eat meals smuggled in knapsacks
by friendly students,
listen to Vivaldi on the ground floor
at the bank of turntables with headphones,
lounge in Periodicals
with the daily paper and a bootleg TV
after closing time,
race up and down the stairwells
to raise my pulse,
collect my mail at the Circulation Desk:

> *Everyone is fine. The washer broke. What*
> *should I use for diaper rash? When are you*
> *coming home?*

JOSEPH SLEEPS,

his eyelids like a moth's fringed wings.
Arms flail against the Ninja Turtle sheet
and suddenly-long legs
race time.

Awake, he's a water-leak detector, a recycling ranger
who bans Styrofoam and asks for beeswax
crayons, a renewable resource.
He wants to adopt the Missouri river,
write the president
to make factories stop polluting.

They're old friends, he and George Bush.
He writes and scolds
the president, every month or so,
about bombing the children of Iraq
(he made his own sign to carry in protest),
about the plight of the California condor and northern gray wolf,
about more shelters and aid for the homeless.
The lion-shaped bulletin board in his room
is covered with pictures and letters from George,
who must be nice,
even if he is a slow learner.

Joseph is a mystery fan, owns 54 Nancy Drews.
Nancy's his friend, along with Jo, Meg, and Amy
and poor Beth, of course, whom he still mourns.
He also reads of knights and wizards, superheroes,
and how to win at Nintendo.

The cats and houseplants are his to feed and water,
and the sunflower blooming in the driveway's border
of weeds. He drew our backyard to scale,
using map symbols, sent off to have it declared
an official wildlife refuge, left a good-night
note on my pillow, written in Egyptian hieroglyphs.

In my life, I have done one good thing.

LOOKING FOR COTTONWOODS

King of lost causes,
champion of the hopeless,
you want to plant a cottonwood
before you die.
"That cotton gets in air conditioners,"
says your landlady, "messes up cars.
Just ruined my good spike heels one year.
Cottonwood's a pest tree."

"Why?" I ask. No naturalist
but expert windmill-tilter,
you describe these natives
of creekbanks and hills greeting settlers
whose descendants cheer their disappearance.
We search for the source
of the cottonwood down blowing from Brush Creek,
but neither of us knows one branch shape
or leaf from another.

To learn acacia from mimosa, linden from locust,
we stroll Loose Park, book in hand,
comparing leaves, flowers, fruits, bark,
naming maple, mulberry,
sycamore, black walnut,
English oak, American elm,
those who waited with the Indians all those centuries,
those the Europeans imported to ornament
a continent of forests
when a squirrel could travel from the Atlantic
to the Missouri without touching the ground.
We take home single- and multi-lobed leaves,

read how fashionable Kansas Citians plant
Bradford pear, vulnerable to every disease and pest.
The cottonwood's invulnerable,
except to lightning and humans.

We walk blocks condemned for the public
benefit of building luxury condos,
the fight against this your latest lost cause.
Cottony down shrouds the vacant houses
and raw earth. By the parked bulldozers,
sitting on an island of grass and tree
within an excavation, roots exposed,
stands the source, fifty feet tall,
the plains cottonwood.
Drifts of gauze dotted with hard kernels
line the edges of the block-long hole.
I seize a handful
to wrap in a tissue
and shelter in your pocket.
At home, I fill a can with damp earth.
We'll keep it inside while it sprouts
so the neighbors can't see,
cottonwood radicals.

SURVIVOR

He is the first, and if you're young enough,
you don't realize it's wrong, and even if you do,
there's the traitor, pleasure, and love
since, after all, he's not some stranger beast
bloodying you in an alley but one of the most important
people in your life, your uncle, your brother,
my father, a sanctuary in life's wilderness.

Then you grow old enough to know the wrong,
not just the sick, hesitant feeling but a fist
to the stomach, a screaming inside
your head, "bad, dirty, shame, sin."
Usually this is about the time you start bleeding,
and your beast wants to move from fondling
and fellatio to full penetration.
Tired of being a scavenger, a hyena,
he wants the full hunt,
and if you're lucky, you fight
so he has to force you (still,
guilt and shame devour you).

For years you run from one to another,
all his species,
all charismatic and cruel,
playing out the same sad chase and kill
(or you flinch any time a man's gaze
rests on your face or body, frozen
like a rabbit facing a fox).
Then one day you decide to stop crazy love,
and you settle for safety,
comfort, refuge.

For years you heal until
you're standing still
at the beginning
where you should have been
without that early abduction
that left you
lost in the dark woods
among the carnivores.

Ready to finally step onto the road
you should have traveled in your youth,
you're waylaid by another smiling predator,
but finally old enough,
strong enough, able to save yourself
(at the cost of all your skin
and one chamber of your heart), you swear off
love and sex and men.

There can be happy endings.
If you're stubborn enough,
you could meet a gentle villager
with fine strong bones and hands
that heat the cold scar-flesh,
take turns crying in each other's arms,
take turns as pursuer and pursued,
take turns healing each other with blinding
new passion that makes you cry out,
yes, and chases away all guilt and shame,
love the way it was supposed to be
before the jackal tore it.

THE MAN WHO DOESN'T WANT ME

Today, I had coffee with the man who doesn't want me.
We sat out on the patio under
the building overhang to avoid the sun,
though there was nothing we could do about the heat.

Conversation and coffee and unconsummated love,
what hot, bitter concoctions we crave.
There was music and icy air inside with the people,
but we didn't want other people, maybe
for different reasons. Sweat slid down my spine
while he kept his sunglasses on the entire time.

I missed his eyes so much I could have blotted out
the fiery sun to bring them back to my own. But he
avoided mine this time, having lingered with them
too long last time we met, perhaps.

Today, his eyes wore shields.
I had no weapons, but he was armored somehow,
as he sat with white cotton shirt covering dark arms,
as if I were a mailed host come against him,
true threat to oppose.

Our talk was small and funny,
and I laughed through the lump in my throat
as we competed for worst neighbors and compared memories
of similar and known pasts.

The future bears no thinking about.
This moment, replaying
in my mind over and over, until I've squeezed

all possible pleasure from it, this moment
in the blinding flare of sun is all
I have to hope for.

Still, a hot surge of joy
fills me when I think of him
alive and part of my world.

MOTH SONG

How many summer evenings have I watched moths
flutter around a candle, inexorably
drawn against their tiny wills
to the very fire that poses greatest danger
to their survival?
How often have I shaken my head
and laughed at their foolhardiness
as they drop with scorch marks on their wings
and crawl feebly still toward the flame
that spells searing death?

Now the moths are revenged
as I circle your flame, mesmerized,
against my intelligence and will
drawn to the danger you are
to my sanity and survival.
I know better, of course; I'm no child
but a full-grown adult
who's finally found my wings
after great struggle.

I know better
than to risk them in the burning
that is your touch, but even as I fall,
scorched, I know I will find myself crawling
still toward your heat and light
to the ghostly whisper of moth laughter.

BE STRONG OF HEART

1

Heart is the ripped and mended plaything
of the young and foolish years,
grimy and worn but stubborn
about clinging to existence.

2

Heart is the principal muscle of the body,
and like all muscles, use strengthens it,
but without exercise, it atrophies and fails.

3

Heart needs to be regularly forced
above the everyday rhythms
to keep its tone and strength.

4

Heart is the thing that keeps beating,
even when we're asleep or unconscious
or drunk or drugged or so sad and hurt
we wish it would stop.

5

Heart is the gift and the giver
in one smooth, double-cycled movement.

6

Heart is the darkest continent, unmapped and dangerous
in the interior, which is why we too often
stay on the surface,
safe from the wild center

7

Heart is the eternal potlatch,
blankets spread open and loaded
with food and durables, the wealth
of the tribe circulating freely.

8

Heart is always at the mercy
of all our baser instincts,
but fear is its greatest enemy.

9

Heart is the real power
creating and giving life,
and all kinds of death
are nothing but failures of heart.

10

Heart is what goes on,
even when the pain is greatest,
because it knows what body and brain forget,
that simply enduring
is the ultimate victory.

LANCELOT AND GUINEVERE—AGAIN.

This time, Lance is a burly farm boy,
bright enough to know he wants something
more than the rich smell of new-mown hay
and the dust that fills eyes and nostrils
and mats against the sweat on his bare torso.
Gwen is a flower child, running away
from horrors at home that make the Hell's Angels,
pimps, and dealers around her seem kind.
No escape since they've imbedded claws
in her psyche and ride her,
even as she flees.

Watch them through years and decades
as they draw closer, unwitting
pawns of their own encoded fates,
he moving from victory to victory
in a career of academic jousts,
she moving from loss to loss—
heartache caused and suffered—
in a career of emotional bouts.
Finally, Gwen's found sanctuary
in a good king's arms, but here comes his pal,
Lance the shining hero,
finally awakening
to the futility of always winning.

Is this love or war
or a little of both?
Who will win?
Virtuous king? Heroic knight? Romantic queen?
Was this always such a cliché,
even the first time around?

I SAID I WOULD GIVE YOU WINGS

I will make them from the cerulean scales of butterflies,
the shine of the sun's rays on falling water,
the sound of cicadas crying their love or loneliness,
the heat radiating from miles of cracked concrete,
the salt in the sweat drying on the softest of my skin,
the improvisational, ever-changing jazz of the mockingbird,
the shade of the widest-spreading, creek-draining cottonwood,
the soft nesting churr of the buff-feathered mourning dove,
the ache of sun-scoured blue skies in the tender, naked eye,
the sensuous curve of your mouth as it smiles against its will,
the slip of pure, clear water, ice-chilled, down the throat,
the first, faint shade of moon in the indigo evening air,
the fireflies blinking codes of lust and love and generation,
the still, jasmine-scented, moisture-heavy midnight air,
the silky, scarlet, moth-borne touch of my heart's devotion.

And you will leap into the air and soar out of sight,
visiting the planets and stars and distant galaxies
to lose your earth-born, manmade pain.
Under the night sky, I will search for your shadow
in the swooping, feather-lifting flight
of every swallow, nighthawk, and owl.

Let me give you wings.

LIKE PROMETHEUS,

you snatched the fire of the gods
to throw on the page and warm
the lonely souls of the rest of us.
Daring outlaw of image and trope,
you lived on the edges on weeds and beetles,
hiding from the vengeance of the mad,
jealous gods of this sick world.

I would wield my love like a knife
to cut the ropes that bind
and tie you to the jagged rock
where the blood-headed vulture,
bred from the rape of your heart
by this brute of a world,
lands to gouge out chunks of your soul.
I would rescue you,
live in chains to set you free.

In the spaces of sanity and healing
before the carrion bird returns,
find a way to throw off your cut bonds
and flee that barren boulder.
I will stay behind and hide your tracks,
lead the chase astray like a mother killdeer
until you are safely hidden
in the wild lands,
untouched by the sellers' gods,
safe in the Mother's embrace.

The rotting smell
of the giant beak

closes in on me,
the sharp rock
against my arched back.
Some fire must be stolen,
and some fire must be rescued.

QUESTIONING AN OLD PHOTO ALBUM

Who are these strange, dated faces
staring at me in black and white,
hand-inked labels hemorrhaged
into oblivion, images
hoarded against the passing
of time and this most dreaded fate,
the fading of memory?

We should not need names,
identifying ghosts of our bursting,
full-to-the-brim days,
when we bled life and passion,
that heartbeat of "everything matters, everything
holds your life in its grasp
for good or ill
forever."

This princely face smiles at me
with confidence in his unforgettable
appeal, always younger now
than my own son who develops
with the years, not frozen in adolescent glory
and arrogance of muscle and charm
like this boy whose name I no longer recall,
although I loved him
with that white-knuckled desperation
that pounds in your brain's ebb and flow —
"He is the answer
to the question of my life!"

I've forgotten
the answer.
I've forgotten
or lost or given away
the question.

FOR MY HUSBAND, SICK

While the wild winds break the trees around us,
piling wooden corpses higher than our heads,
leafy walls beneath drifts of premature snow and ice
to hold unseasonal violence from us,
I hold your body under the covers—though it burns
my hands—give what comfort I can
in the hidden language of skin to skin, caress and stroke
and hold fast against nightmare and fever
alike, my hands the rope
that keeps the tent, the balloon, the sign
from flying away in the vicious gusts.

Sleep, don't worry, try to rest.
When the pull to the infinite
sky becomes too intense
with all your strength to cling
to the familiar burned away,
I will be your wire, your stake;
I'll hold you to our bed
with my own heavy limbs
thrown over your lightening form.

THE SUN GROWS IN YOUR SMILE

When you smile, the air grows warm and soft,
the earth is watered with gentle mists,
seeds sprout and spread leaves above the dark, damp soil,
earthworms pierce the crust and frolic across the surface
to the delight of fat, happily hunting robins,
lilies of the valley unfurl beside purple, grape-scented irises,
fat pink and maroon peonies, and gay California poppies,
damask roses hurl their rich fragrance to the wind,
the crazy-with-sheer-joy song of the Northern mockingbird
echoes above other chirps and sweet winged notes,
gardeners join the worms in the warm, rich dirt,
children gallop across yards and grab handfuls of dandelions
to present to mothers who will set them in glasses of water
in kitchen windows or on dining room tables, weeds
glorious after the dark of winter with the color of the sun
that grows and warms and heals in your smile.

ENOUGH

I dress in the dark,
sneak out and drive
to The Bend In The River
Where Herons Hunt.

As my grandmother taught,
I welcome day with cornmeal
thrown to the directions of the winds,
watch with geese and mallards
and shy wood ducks emerging
as the growing sun lifts
mists from the slow-moving water
where two herons materialize
to stalk the shallows
for swift-darting prey.

And blessing descends
as I sing the day into being,
washing away the pain
of unwanted love.
The world dances around me,
and I move, unthinking,
with its rhythm, one
with tree and cloud and river,
fish and turtle and crow.
Sun melts grief with night's mist—
and the voice of the heron.

"Be river. Be turtle.
Listen to oak and maple,
the wisdom of First Cousins.
Tears of shame,

these are the white way.
Be *Tsalagi* again.
It is the People's nature to love,
as it is the heron's to hunt,
the crow's to seek carrion.
How can we be humiliated
by being who we truly are?"

The dance is broken
by a blaring car radio.
Three laughing, cursing men
pull fishing tackle,
folding chairs, beer coolers
from their trunk, leaving
doors open, radio blasting.
Herons take flight,
wing-shadows passing over me,
wi tsa to li gi,
slow-motion blessings.
I turn to leave this place
these men know by another name.

It is enough to know
the real world dances yet
behind the curtain
of this one.
It is enough that you exist
for me to love
as is my nature.
It is enough.

SHE TURNS HER BACK ON HEATHCLIFF
TO WALK THE MOORS ALONE

Though she flees
demands and domination,
into the haunted land alone,
determined never to surrender
again, never to go soft
and submissive with passion
and the knowledge of another's need,
still she finds it hard
to walk in the winds
of this new world of desire
without ownership or control,
when desperate demand has been the only
means of conveying love —
or what passed for it. She is not ready
for a man who allows her
to come and go, willing
to set her free. She knows
the treachery of peat bogs that imitate
safe ground. Like a moorhen
hiding in the heather,
she is wary of the snare, yet
how can she know she is desired
if her lover does not snatch and seize?

Now she has what she wants
and wonders if she could really need
the crazy, mean
"My woman, mine."
She fights the impulse
to pull back, seek the harsh

old ways with some Heathcliff
who'll want to make her
his, instead of this gentle
lover who'll never make or take
but only give.
She's cried out for this
all her life. Now,
she finds the footing
trickier than she dreamed.

Cross over. Find conviction within
without some macho melodrama
to shore up sense of self.
Find your footing
among the stony grasses.
Learn to stand
in different winds,
to walk alone
with a companion soul
at the corner of your eye,
rather than wrestling
through life with a jealous bear
who wants you
to show the way almost as much
as he wants to devour you.

HEART'S MIGRATION

Setting out to a destination, unknown
but desired and dreamed. Not sure which way
to go. Just following instinct, like migrating hawks
or monarch butterflies, trusting the universe
will see me through the perils, circling the globe
blindly. Prevailing winds push and pull me
from my line of flight until I alight on a branch
or the leaf of a sturdy shrub, pull inward and find
the pulse of passion, the true magnetic pull,
that sets me on my course once more
headed to the place I need to be so much
I will set my self at risk to arrive.

How many times do I swear off the mission?
No more. Storm-beaten, muscles aching,
wings frayed, heart torn, predators hunting.
Nothing can be worth this, I cry and fall
to the nearest perch, where I clean ice
from feathers and rest only long enough
for that constant internal signal
to come in clearly and lure me back
to the hopeless trek over hostile seas and deserts.

Of course, we know the end of this story.
Hawks and monarchs make their dangerous flight
in the thousands every year, even as humans
make it harder and harder for them to survive.
But scientists who track them record
the not inconsiderable numbers
that fail to survive the journey.
So I wing my way across the cloud-tossed sky

toward a place I'm not even sure exists
except in my imagination and my heart —
unless my flight on faith alone is enough
to bring love's sanctuary into being.

ANOTHER ODYSSEUS RETURNS

I don't know what I expected —
that you would greet me with tears and kisses?
But right away I saw
there's no place for me now.

I have believed in your love
all these wandering years,
when I couldn't believe in the gods
or myself.
How could you give what I fled
to someone else?

I could face threats of blood and battle
and the terrors that destroyed my crew —
Scylla, Charybdis, all the rest —
adrenaline rushing power and excitement
through me time after time to meet the test.

But the challenge of holding
to only you, to one spot on the map,
one life, prisoner of Eros,
linked with the welfare of another
(unlike my crew, whose deaths for my pride
and errors stirred no grief or guilt),
that terrified.

Still, always in the back of my mind,
lurked your smile, your soft arms,
the sound of your voice,
knowledge that home waited
within those arms for the day
I grew tired of running.

You smile at him now like the happy wife you are.
All that time I consoled myself
in self-inflicted dangers and discomforts
with thoughts of your tears of longing.
How long did you grieve what had been?
How dare you choose to be
other than what I left?

WALKING ON ICE

after a back injury is a constant
putting yourself at risk.
I know this fear well
from years of setting nerve-damaged heel
firmly on glazed cement
that may turn banana peel on me
as if in some eternal silent film gag.
For you, it's all new —
the discovery that solid earth can shift
you from upright to supine
as soon as the water on its surface hardens.
We age by learning
such hard truths, move through life
gingerly testing our footing, or else
by smashing the brittle in our way
and sweeping the shards
from the sidewalk.
It's not so hard, learning
to balance on the shine.

I AM STILL ALIVE

I had doubted the possibility
when the pain was worst,
choking on tears I had to hide,
forced silence, love denied.

"I am on earth would I be here
if you were not also,"
the poet Eluard wrote.
And I know he knew my heart.

I am water and you are earth
and there is no sky between us,
only fire and ashes
and the bitter taste of burning.

I am a pillar of salt
from turning back to see
one last time the beloved
I am not allowed.

I am the empty cup,
poured out in waste
upon the ground, wine staining
the dirt it moistens like blood.

I am still alive, and I hope —
hope that is life, without expectation,
sense or reason. After all,
I am still alive.

HOW TO BE ALONE IN LOVE

Hold fast, first.
Continue to give,
even when no one wants
what you offer. The power, the wonder
is in the giving.
Call yourself out of yourself,
shedding old skins.
Stripping bare to organ and bone,
open the heart's vein
and give your blood. Commit
and continue to commit.
These choices are always yours.
Be love's fool.
Become God's.
He will understand.
He too loved immoderately.

SCHEHEREZADE IN THE COFFEE SHOP

The man I can't have
gave me tea and poems
and took my stories
and my heart. My dreams
are small and sad. He's always
walking away, deaf
to my cries, as darkness moves
around me. Awake, I smile and do
my conversational dance
to amuse, please, make him laugh
till his smile and eyes fill the room
with golden light. I play
Scheherezade, doling out my stories
like pearls or bright gems into his hands
where they collect for a gleaming
instant before falling through his fingers
to pile at his feet. I know
all that keeps me alive, keeps him
from turning my nightmare all too real,
is the necklace of my life
that I'm dismembering
to give to him moment by moment,
stringing such a fragile sparkling shield
against the headsman's axe.

LOVE'S DEEP LABOR

The painful, heavy work's done.
We've cut most of the brush and vines
back to the dark soil.
Now, it's just a matter of digging out
the envious roots, destroying their talent
for phoenix-like resurgence.
Only then can we plant
new beds and borders, food and flowers.
Once planted, those plots
must be inspected
often and weeded ruthlessly.
No mercy.
No trace, no leaf,
no infant mulberry,
honeysuckle or creeper can be allowed
to surface and live.
It can't be temporary vigilance.
Like coastal patrols in time of war,
we must keep watch against rumors and fears
as much as against enemy boats.

That wild, sweet-blossomed tangle bides its time,
fleshy roots like blind white tentacles
underground too deep
to find the source, waiting
for a week's or month's inattention,
busy with something else —
there's always something else
to insist on attention in the urgent now —
to allow them to surface
in shadowy corners, hidden

from the quick glance,
where they won't be noticed
until it's too late
and the frightening vigor
of entropy chokes and strangles
all dreams of new growth.

MEDITATION ON THE WORD *NEED*

The problem with words of emotion
is how easily meaning drains
from their fiddle-sweet sounds
and they become empty instruments.
I can say *love*
and mean desire to give —
open-handed, open-hearted —
or I am drawn to the light
shining from your soul —
or my life is empty without you —
or I want to run my hands
and mouth down the length of you —
or all of these at once.

Need, now, is a plain word.
I need a nail to hang this picture.
I need money to pay my bills.
I need air and light,
water and food,
shelter from storm and sun and cold.
To be healthy,
to be sane,
to survive,
I need you.

SHE WANTS

to live out her life with this good man,
funny and comfortable.
She wants
a peaceful last half of her life.
Is that too much to ask when she's survived
tempests, shipwrecks, sharks,
time spent in the underworld
wandering with hopeless wraiths?
She wants
no more storms of passion in this protected cove,
pleasure and partnership only.
She wants
June forever.

Into this eternal summer's day comes a green sky,
strangely lit, and winds
that scour the earth with blackened rags of cloud
until trees touch the ground around her
and the lagoon's waters swell into choppy whitecaps.
She wants
to close her eyes and find her still waters
and still air and sun and summer standing still,
holding time and age and desire
and all mortal things at bay.
She wants
it all to go away.

The air smells like rain and thunder.
Will he come to her this time
as a bull or a swan or a shower of gold?
She desires

none of his illusions.
How will he deceive and seduce her
in this incarnation and set her blood on fire?
She wants
never to burn again.
When his winds have whipped her
flame into the storm-darkened sky,
will he leave her
to be drenched and drowned,
battered by the barrier reef?
His shadow blots out summer and sanity,
even with her eyes clenched shut.
She wants ...

NIGHTS ARE ANOTHER COUNTRY

in my house. Days we're ordinary,
affectionate, a close,
happy couple, but nights
require a passport and serious
immunizations, warnings about
security and guerilla attacks.
You are a foreign ruler,
quite possibly benevolent
in intention—but we know how
these things always play out,
don't we?—with needs alien
to and hostile to your citizenry,
me, without power
except to say, "No more,"
and hope to survive
the fallout from the battles
in the streets. Days, we're
the peaceful, devoted
pair all our friends envy.
Nights are always tense
around the DMZ that is our bed
with occasional forays into the bush
where the enemy is always lying
in wait. Sleep is hard, fearful
and troubled. I dream us
going down in flames.

THE ENVIRONMENTALISTS BURN THE PRAIRIE

I abandon,
like Aeneas, fleeing their set fire,
as if from Dido
and chaos, passionate
and fertile as the void was fertile
enough in Genesis to spawn life
down to the last
caterpillar-chewed leaf.

I surrender
when the burning grass falls around me
as the hot winds surge and fail.
Wrapped in a tangle
of pea-vines and walled in
by man-high grass, I welcome
the roar and the smoke and the flame
too much, I fear.

I circle
behind the fireline
and walk on steaming cinders
where a world had been.
Because of the flames, they tell me,
in spring the gayfeather will shoot up
and a thousand tiny orchids will hide
among the roots of renewed grasses.

I escape
to plant my Roman garden in the spring
in measured, lawful rows.
In classic tradition, I limit creation
to that scrap
I control.

NETS

You will climb the lichen-slick rocks,
past ever-thinning cloud layers,
and treeline and snowline, up
into thinner ethers, breathing labored,
to the pinnacle above the world

And spreading your arms like wings
of song, you will leap from the top
of the world and soar for a brief second
above the dirt and pain of the climb
before you begin to sink,
retracing your ascent in reverse,
accelerating as you drop toward
the dusty plain below

Where I will wait, weaving nets
of finest fibers, baby-soft
and steel-strong, handspun from my heart's
longing for your dreams to come true,
running from tree to tree, standing pillars
of the world's past, First Cousins
of our race, begging their power
to stand and hold for my nets of love

Where you will land at last,
windburned and too astonished to see
my hand behind the knots
that hold you from the ground below,
gasping for breath and life to go on

And after, you will lick the salt
of love's tears and sweat from my eyes
and drink deep from the flagon of my heart,

only to fall into sleep, our limbs entangled
as if forgetting which body owns which,
and while you dream of flight, I will dream also

Of weaving ever larger and stronger nets
to gather breezes and winds from across the land,
tying them up and storing them for the day
when I can set them free as you begin your drop
to buoy you up and float you over the earth,
flying free forever from the pain of the ground,
wafted by my woven prayers of desire and devotion
to some new world beyond the clouds,
beyond the reach of my captured winds
and the nets of my love.

GHOSTS

I saw the god in you.
Who knows what you saw in me.
A bull's-eye.
A fish in a barrel.
We lurched along like Dr. Dolittle's legendary beast.

At highest noon,
sun at zenith
in summer's worst heat,
I think of you,
trying to sweat you out of me.

When I tried to leave,
you wouldn't let me.
When I tried to stay,
you wouldn't let me.
You made a ghost of me.

Once you lived on the streets,
no other home, for two hungry weeks.
Once I smashed a lamp
over the head of a Hell's Angel.
Once we trusted each other.

I called you gorgeous.
You called me wonderful.
I called you mean.
I said we brought out the worst in each other.
You called me wrong.

Something in you wouldn't accept love.
You could only want me
when you couldn't have me.
The only way I could keep your love
was to go away forever.

Out of synch with each other,
ghosts of our earlier selves
roam that seaside city.
Tell me, love,
do I haunt you?

ACKNOWLEDGMENTS

I would like to thank Catherine Anderson, José Faus, Andrés Rodríguez, and Trish Reeves, fine poets themselves, who read these poems and made suggestions for revisions on some of them.

"Abishag," "After Dinner Under Van Gogh's *Starry Night*," "After the Final Scene," "Apache Dance In Loose Park," "Blame It On Summer," "Born Again," "Caveat Emptor," "Change Of Gods," "Christmas Eve Meditation Wile Waiting To Pay," "Considering Oceans," "Glenda's Prescription," "In The Beginning," "Meeting Hecate," "Reading At Night," "Self-Portrait As Adam," "Self-Portrait As Burning Bush," "Self-Portrait As Eve," "Self-Portrait As Orpheus And Eurydice," "Skin Hunger," "Steeling Myself," "Susannah," "Text," "Three O'Clock In The Morning, Alone," "To A Lone Dolphin," "Water From The Moon," and "Winning The Battle" all appeared in the chapbook, *Skin Hunger* (Potpourri Publications).

In addition, the author appreciates the following publications where some of these poems have appeared.

The Corner Restaurant Anthology (Wheel Of Fire Press), "Storm Son," (in slightly different form) and "In The Beginning."
Crooked Roads, "I Could Live In The Library."
Dinner Hour, "After Dinner Under Van Gogh's *Starry Night*," "Dreaming Of My Late Mother-In-Law's House," "Making Enchiladas," "Susannah."
Downgo Sun, "Instincts," "The Amazon River Dolphin."
Frontier Report, "In The Beginning," "Joanne's Brain."
Kansas City Star, "Coyote Winter."
New Letters, "Reading At Night."
Potpourri, "Oklahoma Poem," "Three O'Clock In The Morning, Alone," "The Environmentalists Burn The Prairie."
Present Magazine, "Fire Is The Oldest Wild Thing," "Ghosts," "Knitting In Time Of Crisis," "Making Enchiladas."
Primera Página: Poetry from the Latino Heartland (Scapegoat Press), "Three O'Clock In the Morning, Alone," "P.O.W.," "I Said I Would Give You Wings," and "Ghosts."

Radicals, Ruffians, and Outcasts: A Poets for Peace And Justice Anthology
(Wheel Of Fire Press), "I Could Live In The Library,"
"The Environmentalists Burn The Prairie," "Reading At Night."
Wheelhouse Magazine, "Looking For Cottonwoods" and "Survivor."
Z Miscellaneous, "Caveat Emptor," "I Could Live In The Library,"
"Katherine Anne Porter, Implacable," "To A Lone Dolphin."